FANCY FLOWERS

Hand Embroidery Patterns

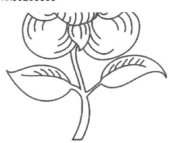

StitchX Embroidery

Supplies you will need to complete this embroidery pattern:

◊ Muslin fabric of any item you wish to stitch on

◊ Needle

◊ Transfer method of your choice

◊ Embroidery floss in the color (or colors) you desire

And of course, bring your creativity!

Our embroidery patterns are designed in a line art style. Many embroiderers choose to stitch the entire design in one color (for example, red for redwork), but others enjoy a more colorful design style. Feel free to make this creation your own! We especially enjoy using hand dyed (variegated) flosses for an extra special look!

Contact us at: stitchxembroidery@gmail.com
Visit our website: www.stitchx.com

©StitchX Embroidery

Embroidery Basics

Most people are familiar with stitches that are used in embroidery. The embroidery craft stitches are the easiest and the more common stitches. The stitches used are thought of by the experts in embroidery as one of the smallest things that is related to this craft. The patterns used in embroidery being made by repeating them or changing them.

The stitches used in embroidery are completed in two ways. The first types of stitches are the hand sewing method and the other is known as the stab method.

In the method of hand sewing, the stitches used in embroidery are created by putting the needle in and bringing it upside of the fabric used in embroidery. The stitch is accomplished by putting the needle in the fabric and pushing it back up to the top again in one move. The thread is then pulled through the fabric to give it a look of plain stitching.

The stab technique of embroidery is made when the needle is put in the material at a ninety degree angle. It is pulled through and the needle is put through under the fabric back to the top. The thread finishing this will be the end of the stitch.

Both of these types of techniques for stitches are very easy for you to do. You can finish them in little time. You can use these basic stitches to complete other stitches with some of them being harder and some of them being easy. Those stitches are listed below and are some of the more common ones to use.

The straight stitch is made when you put the needle in the fabric with an up and down movement. The more common types of this stitch is known as a satin stitch, a fern stitch, a running stitch, a Bosnian and double stitch, and an Algerian stitch.

Back stitches are not like straight stitches. The back stitch is passed the fabric in a round motion. The needle is inserted so that it is coming through the back side of the material and to the right and back through again. The needle will then be reinserted in the back of the fabric and go behind the first stitch you made and then show up in front of the fabric on the left side of the other stitch. These stitches are completed by repetition.

Chain stitching is the type of stitch that works to get a loop of thread on the top of the fabric. You can chain stitch by putting the needle in the fabric at one end of the stitch. The needle is then put into the same place and pushed through the other end of the stitch. The thread is then looped and pulled thought the material.

The cross stitch is one of the more popular types of stitches in embroidery. It is completed by making one diagonal stitch that goes one way and then crossing it with another stitch in the other direction to make an "x" pattern.

Many other stitches for embroidery are out there. Feather stitches, blanket stitches, and buttonhole stitches are among them. You can also learn the couching stitch, the laid stitch, the bullion knot stitch, the knotted stitch and the French knot stitch.

Methods for Transferring Your Designs To Fabric

Transfer Pens And Pencils

These inexpensive tools enable you either to trace a design onto paper, then iron the design onto your fabric (yielding a mirror image), or to draw directly onto your fabric. Some are designed to wash out of the fabric after stitching. Others leave marks which intentionally fade after a brief period of time (from eight to 48 hours) to use when you know you will have sufficient time to complete the stitching. Manufacturers offer various colors of pencils and pens to enable you to transfer onto both light and dark fabrics.

Direct Tracing

If the design fabric is light in color and weight, it's often possible to place the fabric over the design outline and draw directly onto the fabric, using a fabric marking pen. The marks then wash out when the stitching is completed. Always test wash the fabric before transferring.

Dressmaker's Carbon

This allows you to transfer a mirror image of a design onto fabric.

Pricking and Pouncing

This is one of the oldest methods of design transfer, and requires a sharp needle (the eye end may be inserted into a wine cork to make it easier to handle) or tracing wheel to pierce the design paper and either pounce powder, tailor's chalk, or a fabric marking pen. This method is popular with quilters, so you can find supplies for this method at quilting shops